50 Strawberry and Banana Recipes for Home

By: Kelly Johnson

Table of Contents

- Strawberry Banana Smoothie
- Strawberry Banana Pancakes
- Banana Strawberry Muffins
- Strawberry Banana Yogurt Parfait
- Strawberry Banana Ice Cream
- Banana Strawberry Oatmeal
- Strawberry Banana Bread
- Strawberry Banana Smoothie Bowl
- Banana Strawberry Jam
- Strawberry Banana Cheesecake
- Strawberry Banana Pudding
- Strawberry Banana Protein Shake
- Strawberry Banana Scones
- Strawberry Banana Smoothie Popsicles
- Banana Strawberry Salad
- Strawberry Banana French Toast
- Strawberry Banana Cake
- Strawberry Banana Sorbet
- Banana Strawberry Crumble
- Strawberry Banana Overnight Oats
- Strawberry Banana Muffin Bites
- Strawberry Banana Cream Pie
- Strawberry Banana Waffles
- Strawberry Banana Energy Balls
- Banana Strawberry Frozen Yogurt
- Strawberry Banana Chia Pudding
- Strawberry Banana Fritters
- Strawberry Banana Cupcakes
- Strawberry Banana Tarts
- Banana Strawberry Fluff
- Strawberry Banana Pops
- Strawberry Banana Smoothie Muffins

- Banana Strawberry Breakfast Bars
- Strawberry Banana Cheesecake Bars
- Strawberry Banana Bread Pudding
- Strawberry Banana Gelato
- Strawberry Banana Flavored Water
- Strawberry Banana Milkshake
- Strawberry Banana Quinoa Salad
- Strawberry Banana Crepes
- Strawberry Banana Protein Balls
- Strawberry Banana Breakfast Smoothie
- Strawberry Banana Rice Pudding
- Strawberry Banana Crepes
- Strawberry Banana Nut Bars
- Strawberry Banana Jam Bars
- Strawberry Banana Ice Pop
- Strawberry Banana Rice Cake
- Strawberry Banana Granola
- Strawberry Banana Smoothie Cake

Strawberry Banana Smoothie

- 1 cup fresh strawberries, hulled
- 1 banana, peeled
- 1 cup Greek yogurt or milk
- 1 tbsp honey or maple syrup (optional)
- 1/2 cup ice cubes

Instructions:

1. **Blend Ingredients:** In a blender, combine strawberries, banana, Greek yogurt (or milk), and honey.
2. **Add Ice:** Add ice cubes.
3. **Blend:** Blend until smooth and creamy.
4. **Serve:** Pour into glasses and serve immediately.

Strawberry Banana Pancakes

- 1 cup all-purpose flour
- 1 tbsp sugar
- 2 tsp baking powder
- 1/2 tsp salt
- 1 cup milk
- 1 egg
- 2 tbsp melted butter
- 1/2 cup fresh strawberries, sliced
- 1 banana, sliced

Instructions:

1. **Mix Dry Ingredients:** In a large bowl, whisk together flour, sugar, baking powder, and salt.
2. **Combine Wet Ingredients:** In another bowl, mix milk, egg, and melted butter.
3. **Combine:** Pour wet ingredients into dry ingredients and stir until just combined.
4. **Add Fruit:** Gently fold in strawberries and banana slices.
5. **Cook Pancakes:** Heat a non-stick skillet over medium heat and lightly grease. Pour batter onto the skillet and cook until bubbles form on the surface. Flip and cook until golden brown.
6. **Serve:** Serve warm with additional strawberries and bananas on top.

Banana Strawberry Muffins

- 1 cup all-purpose flour
- 1/2 cup sugar
- 1/2 tsp baking soda
- 1/2 tsp baking powder
- 1/4 tsp salt
- 1/2 cup mashed banana (about 1 large banana)
- 1/2 cup chopped fresh strawberries
- 1/4 cup vegetable oil
- 1/4 cup milk
- 1 egg

Instructions:

1. **Preheat Oven:** Preheat oven to 350°F (175°C). Line a muffin tin with paper liners.
2. **Mix Dry Ingredients:** In a large bowl, whisk together flour, sugar, baking soda, baking powder, and salt.
3. **Combine Wet Ingredients:** In another bowl, mix mashed banana, vegetable oil, milk, and egg.
4. **Combine:** Pour wet ingredients into dry ingredients and stir until just combined. Fold in strawberries.
5. **Fill Muffin Tin:** Divide batter evenly among muffin cups.
6. **Bake:** Bake for 20-25 minutes or until a toothpick inserted into the center comes out clean. Cool before serving.

Strawberry Banana Yogurt Parfait

- 1 cup Greek yogurt
- 1/2 cup fresh strawberries, sliced
- 1 banana, sliced
- 1/4 cup granola
- 1 tbsp honey (optional)

Instructions:

1. **Layer Ingredients:** In serving glasses or bowls, layer Greek yogurt, strawberries, banana slices, and granola.
2. **Drizzle Honey:** Drizzle honey over the top if desired.
3. **Serve:** Serve immediately or chill until ready to eat.

Strawberry Banana Ice Cream

- 2 cups fresh strawberries, hulled
- 2 bananas, peeled and sliced
- 1 cup heavy cream
- 1/2 cup sugar
- 1 tsp vanilla extract

Instructions:

1. **Prepare Fruit:** In a blender, combine strawberries, bananas, sugar, and vanilla extract.
2. **Blend:** Blend until smooth.
3. **Mix with Cream:** Add heavy cream and blend until well combined.
4. **Churn:** Pour mixture into an ice cream maker and churn according to the manufacturer's instructions.
5. **Freeze:** Transfer to a container and freeze until firm.

Banana Strawberry Oatmeal

- 1 cup rolled oats
- 2 cups milk (or water)
- 1 banana, sliced
- 1/2 cup fresh strawberries, sliced
- 1 tbsp honey or maple syrup
- 1/4 tsp cinnamon (optional)

Instructions:

1. **Cook Oats:** In a medium saucepan, bring milk (or water) to a boil. Stir in oats, reduce heat, and simmer for 5 minutes, stirring occasionally.
2. **Add Fruit:** Stir in banana slices and strawberries.
3. **Sweeten:** Add honey or maple syrup, and cinnamon if desired.
4. **Serve:** Serve warm.

Strawberry Banana Bread

- 1 1/2 cups all-purpose flour
- 1 tsp baking powder
- 1/2 tsp baking soda
- 1/2 tsp salt
- 1/2 cup butter, softened
- 1 cup sugar
- 2 eggs
- 1/2 cup mashed banana (about 1 large banana)
- 1/2 cup chopped fresh strawberries

Instructions:

1. **Preheat Oven:** Preheat oven to 350°F (175°C). Grease a loaf pan.
2. **Mix Dry Ingredients:** In a bowl, whisk together flour, baking powder, baking soda, and salt.
3. **Cream Butter and Sugar:** In another bowl, cream together butter and sugar until light and fluffy.
4. **Add Eggs and Banana:** Beat in eggs one at a time, then stir in mashed banana.
5. **Combine:** Gradually add dry ingredients to the wet ingredients, mixing until just combined. Fold in strawberries.
6. **Bake:** Pour batter into prepared loaf pan. Bake for 55-60 minutes or until a toothpick inserted into the center comes out clean. Cool before slicing.

Strawberry Banana Smoothie Bowl

- 1 cup fresh strawberries, hulled
- 1 banana, peeled
- 1/2 cup Greek yogurt
- 1/4 cup almond milk (or milk of choice)
- 1 tbsp honey or maple syrup (optional)
- 1/4 cup granola
- Fresh berries and sliced banana for topping

Instructions:

1. **Blend Base:** In a blender, combine strawberries, banana, Greek yogurt, and almond milk. Blend until smooth.
2. **Sweeten:** Add honey or maple syrup if desired and blend briefly to combine.
3. **Serve:** Pour into a bowl and top with granola, fresh berries, and additional banana slices.

Banana Strawberry Jam

- 2 cups strawberries, hulled and chopped
- 2 bananas, peeled and sliced
- 1 cup granulated sugar
- 1 tbsp lemon juice
- 1/2 tsp vanilla extract (optional)

Instructions:

1. **Cook Fruit:** In a large saucepan, combine strawberries, bananas, and sugar. Cook over medium heat, stirring frequently, until the fruit releases its juices and the mixture starts to thicken (about 15-20 minutes).
2. **Add Lemon Juice:** Stir in lemon juice and cook for an additional 5 minutes.
3. **Blend (Optional):** For a smoother texture, blend the mixture using an immersion blender or in batches in a regular blender.
4. **Cool and Store:** Let cool slightly, then transfer to sterilized jars and refrigerate.

Strawberry Banana Cheesecake

- **For the Crust:**
    - 1 1/2 cups graham cracker crumbs
    - 1/4 cup sugar
    - 1/2 cup melted butter
- **For the Filling:**
    - 2 cups cream cheese, softened
    - 1 cup sour cream
    - 1 cup sugar
    - 3 large eggs
    - 1 tsp vanilla extract
    - 1 cup fresh strawberries, chopped
    - 1 banana, sliced
- **For the Topping:**
    - 1/2 cup strawberry jam
    - Fresh strawberries and banana slices

Instructions:

1. **Preheat Oven:** Preheat oven to 325°F (163°C). Grease a springform pan.
2. **Prepare Crust:** Mix graham cracker crumbs, sugar, and melted butter. Press mixture into the bottom of the pan.
3. **Make Filling:** Beat cream cheese, sour cream, and sugar until smooth. Add eggs one at a time, beating well after each addition. Stir in vanilla extract.
4. **Add Fruit:** Gently fold in chopped strawberries and banana slices.
5. **Bake:** Pour filling over crust and bake for 50-60 minutes, or until set. Cool completely.
6. **Add Topping:** Spread strawberry jam over the top. Garnish with fresh strawberries and banana slices.

Strawberry Banana Pudding

- 1 cup milk
- 1/2 cup heavy cream
- 1/2 cup sugar
- 1/4 cup cornstarch
- 1/4 tsp salt
- 2 eggs
- 1 tsp vanilla extract
- 1 cup fresh strawberries, sliced
- 1 banana, sliced

Instructions:

1. **Cook Pudding Base:** In a medium saucepan, whisk together milk, cream, sugar, cornstarch, and salt. Cook over medium heat, stirring constantly, until mixture thickens and starts to boil.
2. **Add Eggs:** Beat eggs in a bowl. Gradually whisk in a small amount of the hot pudding mixture, then return to the pan and cook for 1-2 more minutes, stirring constantly.
3. **Finish:** Remove from heat and stir in vanilla extract. Allow to cool slightly.
4. **Layer Pudding:** In serving dishes, layer pudding with sliced strawberries and banana. Chill before serving.

Strawberry Banana Protein Shake

- 1 cup fresh strawberries, hulled
- 1 banana, peeled
- 1 cup almond milk (or milk of choice)
- 1 scoop vanilla protein powder
- 1 tbsp honey or maple syrup (optional)
- 1/2 cup ice cubes

Instructions:

1. **Blend Ingredients:** In a blender, combine strawberries, banana, almond milk, protein powder, and honey.
2. **Add Ice:** Add ice cubes and blend until smooth.
3. **Serve:** Pour into glasses and enjoy immediately.

Strawberry Banana Scones

- 2 cups all-purpose flour
- 1/4 cup sugar
- 1 tbsp baking powder
- 1/2 tsp salt
- 1/2 cup cold butter, cut into small pieces
- 1/2 cup fresh strawberries, chopped
- 1 banana, mashed
- 1/2 cup milk
- 1 egg

Instructions:

1. **Preheat Oven:** Preheat oven to 400°F (200°C). Line a baking sheet with parchment paper.
2. **Mix Dry Ingredients:** In a large bowl, whisk together flour, sugar, baking powder, and salt.
3. **Cut in Butter:** Cut in cold butter until mixture resembles coarse crumbs.
4. **Add Fruit:** Stir in chopped strawberries and mashed banana.
5. **Mix Wet Ingredients:** In a small bowl, whisk together milk and egg. Add to the flour mixture and stir until just combined.
6. **Shape and Bake:** Turn dough onto a floured surface and shape into a circle. Cut into wedges and place on the baking sheet. Bake for 15-20 minutes, or until golden brown. Cool before serving.

Strawberry Banana Smoothie Popsicles

- 1 cup fresh strawberries, hulled
- 1 banana, peeled
- 1/2 cup Greek yogurt
- 1/4 cup honey or maple syrup
- 1/4 cup milk (or almond milk)

Instructions:

1. **Blend Ingredients:** In a blender, combine strawberries, banana, Greek yogurt, honey, and milk. Blend until smooth.
2. **Pour into Molds:** Pour mixture into popsicle molds.
3. **Freeze:** Insert sticks and freeze for at least 4 hours or until solid.
4. **Serve:** Run under warm water briefly to release popsicles.

Banana Strawberry Salad

- 2 cups mixed greens
- 1 cup fresh strawberries, sliced
- 1 banana, sliced
- 1/4 cup chopped nuts (such as almonds or walnuts)
- 1/4 cup crumbled feta cheese
- 2 tbsp balsamic vinaigrette

Instructions:

1. **Prepare Salad:** In a large bowl, toss mixed greens with strawberries, banana slices, nuts, and feta cheese.
2. **Dress Salad:** Drizzle with balsamic vinaigrette and toss gently to coat.
3. **Serve:** Serve immediately.

Strawberry Banana French Toast

- 4 slices bread (such as brioche or challah)
- 2 eggs
- 1/2 cup milk
- 1/2 tsp vanilla extract
- 1/4 tsp ground cinnamon
- 1 banana, sliced
- 1/2 cup fresh strawberries, sliced
- Butter or oil for cooking
- Maple syrup for serving

Instructions:

1. **Prepare Batter:** In a bowl, whisk together eggs, milk, vanilla extract, and cinnamon.
2. **Dip Bread:** Dip each slice of bread into the egg mixture, ensuring it's well coated.
3. **Cook French Toast:** Heat butter or oil in a skillet over medium heat. Cook bread slices until golden brown on both sides.
4. **Serve:** Top with banana and strawberry slices. Drizzle with maple syrup.

Strawberry Banana Cake

- **For the Cake:**
    - 1 1/2 cups all-purpose flour
    - 1 cup sugar
    - 1 1/2 tsp baking powder
    - 1/2 tsp baking soda
    - 1/4 tsp salt
    - 1/2 cup butter, softened
    - 1/2 cup mashed banana (about 1 large banana)
    - 1/2 cup milk
    - 1/2 cup fresh strawberries, chopped
    - 2 large eggs
- **For the Frosting:**
    - 1/2 cup butter, softened
    - 2 cups powdered sugar
    - 1/4 cup fresh strawberries, pureed
    - 1 tsp vanilla extract

Instructions:

1. **Preheat Oven:** Preheat oven to 350°F (175°C). Grease and flour a cake pan.
2. **Mix Dry Ingredients:** In a bowl, whisk together flour, sugar, baking powder, baking soda, and salt.
3. **Prepare Wet Ingredients:** In another bowl, cream butter until smooth. Add mashed banana and mix well. Beat in eggs one at a time, then stir in milk.
4. **Combine:** Gradually add dry ingredients to the wet ingredients, mixing until just combined. Fold in chopped strawberries.
5. **Bake:** Pour batter into prepared pan and bake for 30-35 minutes or until a toothpick inserted into the center comes out clean. Cool completely.
6. **Prepare Frosting:** Beat butter until creamy. Gradually add powdered sugar, strawberry puree, and vanilla extract. Mix until smooth.
7. **Frost Cake:** Frost cooled cake and garnish with additional strawberries if desired.

Strawberry Banana Sorbet

- 2 cups fresh strawberries, hulled
- 2 bananas, peeled and sliced
- 1/2 cup sugar
- 1/2 cup water
- 1 tbsp lemon juice

Instructions:

1. **Blend Ingredients:** In a blender, combine strawberries, bananas, sugar, water, and lemon juice. Blend until smooth.
2. **Chill Mixture:** Pour mixture into a bowl and refrigerate for 1-2 hours.
3. **Freeze:** Pour into an ice cream maker and churn according to the manufacturer's instructions.
4. **Serve:** Transfer to a container and freeze until firm. Scoop and serve.

Banana Strawberry Crumble

- **For the Filling:**
    - 2 cups fresh strawberries, sliced
    - 2 bananas, sliced
    - 1/4 cup sugar
    - 1 tbsp lemon juice
- **For the Crumble Topping:**
    - 1/2 cup all-purpose flour
    - 1/2 cup rolled oats
    - 1/4 cup brown sugar
    - 1/4 cup cold butter, cut into small pieces
    - 1/4 tsp cinnamon

Instructions:

1. **Prepare Filling:** In a bowl, toss strawberries, bananas, sugar, and lemon juice. Pour into a baking dish.
2. **Make Crumble Topping:** In another bowl, mix flour, oats, brown sugar, and cinnamon. Cut in butter until mixture resembles coarse crumbs.
3. **Assemble and Bake:** Sprinkle topping over fruit filling. Bake at 350°F (175°C) for 30-35 minutes, or until topping is golden brown and fruit is bubbly. Let cool slightly before serving.

Strawberry Banana Overnight Oats

- 1/2 cup rolled oats
- 1/2 cup milk (or almond milk)
- 1/2 cup Greek yogurt
- 1 banana, sliced
- 1/2 cup fresh strawberries, sliced
- 1 tbsp honey or maple syrup
- 1/4 tsp vanilla extract

Instructions:

1. **Combine Ingredients:** In a jar or container, mix oats, milk, Greek yogurt, honey, and vanilla extract.
2. **Add Fruit:** Top with banana and strawberry slices.
3. **Refrigerate:** Cover and refrigerate overnight.
4. **Serve:** Stir before serving and enjoy cold.

Strawberry Banana Muffin Bites

- 1 cup all-purpose flour
- 1/2 cup sugar
- 1/2 tsp baking powder
- 1/4 tsp baking soda
- 1/4 tsp salt
- 1/2 cup mashed banana (about 1 large banana)
- 1/2 cup fresh strawberries, chopped
- 1/4 cup vegetable oil
- 1/4 cup milk
- 1 egg

Instructions:

1. **Preheat Oven:** Preheat oven to 350°F (175°C). Line a mini muffin tin with paper liners.
2. **Mix Dry Ingredients:** In a large bowl, whisk together flour, sugar, baking powder, baking soda, and salt.
3. **Combine Wet Ingredients:** In another bowl, mix mashed banana, vegetable oil, milk, and egg.
4. **Combine:** Pour wet ingredients into dry ingredients and stir until just combined. Fold in strawberries.
5. **Fill Muffin Tin:** Divide batter evenly among mini muffin cups.
6. **Bake:** Bake for 10-12 minutes or until a toothpick inserted into the center comes out clean. Cool before serving.

Strawberry Banana Cream Pie

- **For the Crust:**
    - 1 1/2 cups graham cracker crumbs
    - 1/4 cup sugar
    - 1/2 cup melted butter
- **For the Filling:**
    - 1 cup fresh strawberries, sliced
    - 2 bananas, sliced
    - 1 cup heavy cream
    - 1/2 cup powdered sugar
    - 1 tsp vanilla extract

Instructions:

1. **Preheat Oven:** Preheat oven to 350°F (175°C). Press graham cracker crumbs mixed with sugar and melted butter into a pie dish. Bake for 8-10 minutes. Let cool.
2. **Prepare Filling:** In a bowl, beat heavy cream with powdered sugar and vanilla extract until stiff peaks form.
3. **Assemble Pie:** Layer sliced strawberries and bananas over the cooled crust. Spread whipped cream over the fruit.
4. **Chill:** Refrigerate for at least 2 hours before serving.

Strawberry Banana Waffles

- 1 1/2 cups all-purpose flour
- 2 tbsp sugar
- 1 tbsp baking powder
- 1/2 tsp salt
- 1 1/4 cups milk
- 1/2 cup vegetable oil
- 2 eggs
- 1 banana, mashed
- 1/2 cup fresh strawberries, chopped

Instructions:

1. **Preheat Waffle Iron:** Preheat waffle iron according to manufacturer's instructions.
2. **Mix Dry Ingredients:** In a large bowl, whisk together flour, sugar, baking powder, and salt.
3. **Combine Wet Ingredients:** In another bowl, mix milk, vegetable oil, eggs, and mashed banana.
4. **Combine:** Add wet ingredients to dry ingredients and stir until just combined. Fold in strawberries.
5. **Cook Waffles:** Pour batter into preheated waffle iron and cook until golden brown. Serve warm with your favorite toppings.

Strawberry Banana Energy Balls

- 1 cup rolled oats
- 1/2 cup almond butter
- 1/2 cup mashed banana (about 1 large banana)
- 1/4 cup chopped fresh strawberries
- 1/4 cup honey or maple syrup
- 1/4 cup mini chocolate chips (optional)

Instructions:

1. **Mix Ingredients:** In a bowl, combine oats, almond butter, mashed banana, chopped strawberries, honey, and mini chocolate chips if using.
2. **Form Balls:** Roll mixture into small balls (about 1 inch in diameter).
3. **Chill:** Place on a baking sheet and refrigerate for at least 30 minutes before serving.

Banana Strawberry Frozen Yogurt

- 2 cups Greek yogurt
- 1 cup fresh strawberries, hulled and chopped
- 2 bananas, peeled and sliced
- 1/2 cup honey or maple syrup
- 1 tsp vanilla extract

Instructions:

1. **Prepare Mixture:** In a blender, combine Greek yogurt, strawberries, bananas, honey, and vanilla extract. Blend until smooth.
2. **Churn:** Pour mixture into an ice cream maker and churn according to manufacturer's instructions.
3. **Freeze:** Transfer to a container and freeze until firm. Scoop and serve.

Strawberry Banana Chia Pudding

- 1/4 cup chia seeds
- 1 cup almond milk (or milk of choice)
- 1 banana, mashed
- 1/2 cup fresh strawberries, chopped
- 1 tbsp honey or maple syrup
- 1/2 tsp vanilla extract

Instructions:

1. **Mix Ingredients:** In a bowl, combine chia seeds, almond milk, mashed banana, honey, and vanilla extract.
2. **Refrigerate:** Cover and refrigerate for at least 4 hours or overnight, stirring occasionally.
3. **Serve:** Top with chopped strawberries before serving.

Strawberry Banana Fritters

- 1 cup all-purpose flour
- 1/4 cup sugar
- 1 tsp baking powder
- 1/4 tsp salt
- 1/2 cup mashed banana (about 1 large banana)
- 1/2 cup fresh strawberries, chopped
- 1/4 cup milk
- 1 large egg
- Oil for frying

Instructions:

1. **Prepare Batter:** In a bowl, mix flour, sugar, baking powder, and salt. In another bowl, combine mashed banana, milk, and egg. Add wet ingredients to dry ingredients and stir until just combined. Fold in strawberries.
2. **Heat Oil:** Heat oil in a skillet over medium heat.
3. **Fry Fritters:** Drop spoonfuls of batter into the hot oil and cook until golden brown on both sides, about 2-3 minutes per side. Drain on paper towels.
4. **Serve:** Dust with powdered sugar if desired and serve warm.

Strawberry Banana Cupcakes

- **For the Cupcakes:**
    - 1 1/2 cups all-purpose flour
    - 1 cup sugar
    - 1 1/2 tsp baking powder
    - 1/4 tsp salt
    - 1/2 cup unsalted butter, softened
    - 1/2 cup mashed banana (about 1 large banana)
    - 1/2 cup fresh strawberries, chopped
    - 2 large eggs
    - 1/2 cup milk
    - 1 tsp vanilla extract
- **For the Frosting:**
    - 1/2 cup unsalted butter, softened
    - 1 1/2 cups powdered sugar
    - 2 tbsp milk
    - 1/2 tsp vanilla extract
    - 1/4 cup fresh strawberries, pureed

Instructions:

1. **Preheat Oven:** Preheat oven to 350°F (175°C). Line a muffin tin with paper liners.
2. **Prepare Batter:** In a bowl, whisk together flour, sugar, baking powder, and salt. In another bowl, cream butter until smooth. Add eggs one at a time, mixing well. Stir in mashed banana and milk. Gradually add dry ingredients and mix until just combined. Fold in strawberries.
3. **Bake:** Divide batter among muffin cups and bake for 18-22 minutes, or until a toothpick inserted into the center comes out clean. Cool completely.
4. **Make Frosting:** Beat butter until creamy. Gradually add powdered sugar, milk, vanilla, and strawberry puree, mixing until smooth.
5. **Frost Cupcakes:** Frost cooled cupcakes and garnish with additional strawberries if desired.

Strawberry Banana Tarts

- **For the Tart Crust:**
    - 1 1/2 cups all-purpose flour
    - 1/4 cup sugar
    - 1/2 cup cold butter, cut into small pieces
    - 1 egg yolk
    - 1-2 tbsp cold water
- **For the Filling:**
    - 1 cup fresh strawberries, sliced
    - 1 banana, sliced
    - 1/4 cup strawberry jam

Instructions:

1. **Preheat Oven:** Preheat oven to 375°F (190°C). Grease tart pans.
2. **Make Crust:** In a bowl, mix flour and sugar. Cut in butter until mixture resembles coarse crumbs. Stir in egg yolk and enough cold water to form a dough. Press dough into tart pans.
3. **Bake Crusts:** Bake for 12-15 minutes or until golden. Let cool.
4. **Prepare Filling:** Arrange sliced strawberries and bananas in the cooled tart shells. Heat strawberry jam until liquid and brush over the fruit.
5. **Serve:** Chill before serving.

Banana Strawberry Fluff

- 1 cup fresh strawberries, chopped
- 2 bananas, sliced
- 1 cup marshmallow fluff
- 1 cup whipped cream

Instructions:

1. **Combine Ingredients:** In a bowl, fold marshmallow fluff into whipped cream until well combined.
2. **Add Fruit:** Gently fold in strawberries and banana slices.
3. **Chill:** Refrigerate for at least 1 hour before serving.

Strawberry Banana Pops

- 1 cup fresh strawberries, hulled and chopped
- 2 bananas, peeled and sliced
- 1 cup Greek yogurt
- 1/4 cup honey or maple syrup

Instructions:

1. **Prepare Mixture:** In a blender, blend strawberries, bananas, Greek yogurt, and honey until smooth.
2. **Pour into Molds:** Pour mixture into popsicle molds.
3. **Freeze:** Insert sticks and freeze for at least 4 hours or until solid.
4. **Serve:** Run under warm water briefly to release popsicles.

Strawberry Banana Smoothie Muffins

- 1 1/2 cups all-purpose flour
- 1/2 cup sugar
- 1 tsp baking powder
- 1/2 tsp baking soda
- 1/4 tsp salt
- 1/2 cup mashed banana (about 1 large banana)
- 1/2 cup fresh strawberries, chopped
- 1/2 cup Greek yogurt
- 1/4 cup milk
- 1 egg
- 1/4 cup honey or maple syrup

Instructions:

1. **Preheat Oven:** Preheat oven to 350°F (175°C). Line a muffin tin with paper liners.
2. **Prepare Batter:** In a bowl, mix flour, sugar, baking powder, baking soda, and salt. In another bowl, combine mashed banana, Greek yogurt, milk, egg, and honey. Stir into dry ingredients until just combined. Fold in strawberries.
3. **Bake:** Divide batter among muffin cups and bake for 18-22 minutes, or until a toothpick inserted into the center comes out clean. Cool before serving.

Banana Strawberry Breakfast Bars

- **For the Bars:**
    - 1 1/2 cups rolled oats
    - 1/2 cup all-purpose flour
    - 1/2 cup mashed banana (about 1 large banana)
    - 1/2 cup fresh strawberries, chopped
    - 1/4 cup honey or maple syrup
    - 1/4 cup unsweetened applesauce
    - 1/4 cup chopped nuts (optional)
    - 1/2 tsp vanilla extract
    - 1/2 tsp baking powder

Instructions:

1. **Preheat Oven:** Preheat oven to 350°F (175°C). Line an 8x8 inch baking dish with parchment paper.
2. **Mix Ingredients:** In a bowl, combine oats, flour, baking powder, mashed banana, honey, applesauce, and vanilla extract. Fold in strawberries and nuts if using.
3. **Bake:** Spread mixture evenly in the prepared dish. Bake for 25-30 minutes, or until golden and firm. Let cool before cutting into bars.

Strawberry Banana Cheesecake Bars

- **For the Crust:**
    - 1 1/2 cups graham cracker crumbs
    - 1/4 cup sugar
    - 1/2 cup melted butter
- **For the Filling:**
    - 16 oz cream cheese, softened
    - 1/2 cup sugar
    - 2 large eggs
    - 1/2 cup sour cream
    - 1 tsp vanilla extract
    - 1/2 cup mashed banana (about 1 large banana)
    - 1/2 cup fresh strawberries, chopped

Instructions:

1. **Preheat Oven:** Preheat oven to 325°F (165°C). Line a baking pan with parchment paper.
2. **Prepare Crust:** Mix graham cracker crumbs, sugar, and melted butter. Press into the bottom of the pan.
3. **Prepare Filling:** Beat cream cheese and sugar until smooth. Add eggs one at a time, beating well. Mix in sour cream, vanilla extract, and mashed banana. Fold in strawberries.
4. **Bake:** Pour filling over crust. Bake for 40-45 minutes, or until set. Cool, then chill before slicing.

Strawberry Banana Bread Pudding

- 4 cups cubed bread (day-old or stale)
- 1 cup fresh strawberries, sliced
- 1 banana, sliced
- 2 cups milk
- 3 large eggs
- 1/2 cup sugar
- 1 tsp vanilla extract
- 1/2 tsp ground cinnamon
- 1/4 cup butter, melted

Instructions:

1. **Preheat Oven:** Preheat oven to 350°F (175°C). Grease a baking dish.
2. **Prepare Mixture:** In a bowl, whisk together milk, eggs, sugar, vanilla extract, and cinnamon. Add bread cubes, strawberries, and banana slices. Stir to coat.
3. **Bake:** Pour mixture into the baking dish. Drizzle melted butter over the top. Bake for 45-50 minutes, or until set and golden brown. Let cool slightly before serving.

Strawberry Banana Gelato

- 1 cup fresh strawberries, hulled and chopped
- 2 bananas, peeled and sliced
- 1 cup whole milk
- 1 cup heavy cream
- 1/2 cup sugar
- 1 tsp lemon juice

Instructions:

1. **Prepare Mixture:** In a blender, combine strawberries, bananas, milk, heavy cream, sugar, and lemon juice. Blend until smooth.
2. **Churn:** Pour mixture into an ice cream maker and churn according to manufacturer's instructions.
3. **Freeze:** Transfer to a container and freeze until firm. Serve scooped.

Strawberry Banana Flavored Water

- 1 cup fresh strawberries, sliced
- 1 banana, sliced
- 1 quart water
- Ice cubes (optional)

Instructions:

1. **Combine Ingredients:** In a large pitcher, combine strawberries, banana slices, and water.
2. **Infuse:** Refrigerate for at least 2 hours to let the flavors infuse.
3. **Serve:** Serve over ice if desired.

Strawberry Banana Milkshake

- 1 cup fresh strawberries, hulled
- 2 bananas, peeled
- 1 cup milk
- 1/2 cup vanilla ice cream
- 2 tbsp honey or sugar (optional)

Instructions:

1. **Blend Ingredients:** In a blender, combine strawberries, bananas, milk, vanilla ice cream, and honey if using. Blend until smooth.
2. **Serve:** Pour into glasses and serve immediately.

Strawberry Banana Quinoa Salad

- 1 cup cooked quinoa, cooled
- 1 cup fresh strawberries, chopped
- 1 banana, sliced
- 1/4 cup chopped nuts (such as almonds or walnuts)
- 1/4 cup feta cheese (optional)
- 2 tbsp honey
- 1 tbsp lemon juice

Instructions:

1. **Combine Salad:** In a large bowl, mix quinoa, strawberries, banana, nuts, and feta cheese if using.
2. **Prepare Dressing:** Whisk together honey and lemon juice. Drizzle over the salad and toss gently.
3. **Serve:** Chill before serving.

Strawberry Banana Crepes

- **For the Crepes:**
    - 1 cup all-purpose flour
    - 2 large eggs
    - 1 cup milk
    - 2 tbsp melted butter
    - 1 tbsp sugar
    - 1/4 tsp salt
- **For the Filling:**
    - 1/2 cup fresh strawberries, sliced
    - 1 banana, sliced
    - 2 tbsp honey or maple syrup

Instructions:

1. **Prepare Batter:** In a bowl, whisk together flour, eggs, milk, melted butter, sugar, and salt until smooth. Let batter rest for 30 minutes.
2. **Cook Crepes:** Heat a non-stick skillet over medium heat and lightly grease. Pour in a small amount of batter, swirling to cover the pan. Cook until edges lift and flip to cook the other side. Repeat with remaining batter.
3. **Assemble Crepes:** Fill crepes with sliced strawberries, bananas, and a drizzle of honey or maple syrup. Fold or roll up and serve.

Strawberry Banana Protein Balls

- 1 cup rolled oats
- 1/2 cup almond butter
- 1/2 cup mashed banana (about 1 large banana)
- 1/4 cup chopped fresh strawberries
- 1/4 cup protein powder (vanilla or unflavored)
- 2 tbsp honey or maple syrup
- 1/4 cup mini chocolate chips (optional)

Instructions:

1. **Mix Ingredients:** In a bowl, combine oats, almond butter, mashed banana, chopped strawberries, protein powder, and honey. Stir until well combined. Add mini chocolate chips if using.
2. **Form Balls:** Roll mixture into 1-inch balls.
3. **Chill:** Place on a baking sheet and refrigerate for at least 30 minutes before serving.

Strawberry Banana Breakfast Smoothie

- 1 banana, peeled and sliced
- 1 cup fresh strawberries, hulled
- 1/2 cup Greek yogurt
- 1/2 cup milk
- 1 tbsp honey or maple syrup
- 1/2 cup ice cubes

Instructions:

1. **Blend Ingredients:** In a blender, combine banana, strawberries, Greek yogurt, milk, honey, and ice cubes. Blend until smooth.
2. **Serve:** Pour into glasses and serve immediately.

Strawberry Banana Rice Pudding

- 1/2 cup Arborio rice
- 1 1/2 cups milk
- 1/4 cup sugar
- 1/2 cup fresh strawberries, chopped
- 1 banana, sliced
- 1/2 tsp vanilla extract

Instructions:

1. **Cook Rice:** In a saucepan, combine rice, milk, and sugar. Cook over medium heat, stirring frequently, until rice is tender and mixture is creamy, about 20-25 minutes.
2. **Add Fruit:** Stir in chopped strawberries, banana slices, and vanilla extract. Cook for an additional 5 minutes.
3. **Serve:** Let cool slightly before serving.

Strawberry Banana Nut Bars

- 1 cup rolled oats
- 1/2 cup chopped nuts (such as almonds or walnuts)
- 1/2 cup dried strawberries
- 1/2 cup mashed banana (about 1 large banana)
- 1/4 cup honey or maple syrup
- 1/4 cup almond butter

Instructions:

1. **Preheat Oven:** Preheat oven to 350°F (175°C). Line an 8x8 inch baking dish with parchment paper.
2. **Mix Ingredients:** In a bowl, combine oats, chopped nuts, dried strawberries, mashed banana, honey, and almond butter. Stir until well mixed.
3. **Bake:** Press mixture into the prepared baking dish. Bake for 20-25 minutes, or until golden. Let cool before cutting into bars.

Strawberry Banana Jam Bars

- **For the Crust:**
    - 1 1/2 cups all-purpose flour
    - 1/2 cup sugar
    - 1/2 cup cold butter, cut into small pieces
- **For the Filling:**
    - 1/2 cup fresh strawberries, chopped
    - 1 banana, mashed
    - 1/4 cup sugar
    - 1 tbsp lemon juice
    - 1/2 tsp vanilla extract

Instructions:

1. **Preheat Oven:** Preheat oven to 350°F (175°C). Line an 8x8 inch baking dish with parchment paper.
2. **Prepare Crust:** Mix flour and sugar in a bowl. Cut in butter until mixture resembles coarse crumbs. Press half of the mixture into the bottom of the prepared dish.
3. **Prepare Filling:** In a bowl, mix strawberries, banana, sugar, lemon juice, and vanilla extract. Spread over the crust.
4. **Top Bars:** Sprinkle remaining crumb mixture over the filling. Bake for 30-35 minutes, or until topping is golden. Cool before cutting into squares.

Strawberry Banana Ice Pop

- 1 cup fresh strawberries, hulled and chopped
- 1 banana, peeled and sliced
- 1/2 cup Greek yogurt
- 1/4 cup honey or maple syrup
- 1/4 cup water

Instructions:

1. **Prepare Mixture:** In a blender, combine strawberries, banana, Greek yogurt, honey, and water. Blend until smooth.
2. **Pour and Freeze:** Pour the mixture into ice pop molds. Insert sticks and freeze for at least 4 hours or until solid.
3. **Serve:** Run under warm water briefly to release popsicles.

Strawberry Banana Rice Cake

- 1 cup cooked white or brown rice
- 1/2 cup mashed banana (about 1 large banana)
- 1/2 cup fresh strawberries, chopped
- 1/4 cup honey or maple syrup
- 1/2 tsp vanilla extract

Instructions:

1. **Mix Ingredients:** In a bowl, combine cooked rice, mashed banana, strawberries, honey, and vanilla extract. Mix well.
2. **Form Cakes:** Press mixture into a lined baking dish or mold to shape into rice cakes.
3. **Chill:** Refrigerate for at least 1 hour before cutting into squares or rounds.

Strawberry Banana Granola

- 2 cups old-fashioned oats
- 1/2 cup chopped nuts (such as almonds or walnuts)
- 1/2 cup dried strawberries
- 1/4 cup honey or maple syrup
- 1/4 cup coconut oil
- 1/2 cup mashed banana (about 1 large banana)
- 1/2 tsp vanilla extract

Instructions:

1. **Preheat Oven:** Preheat oven to 350°F (175°C). Line a baking sheet with parchment paper.
2. **Mix Ingredients:** In a bowl, mix oats, nuts, dried strawberries, mashed banana, honey, coconut oil, and vanilla extract.
3. **Bake:** Spread mixture evenly on the baking sheet. Bake for 20-25 minutes, stirring halfway through, until golden brown. Let cool before breaking into clusters.

Strawberry Banana Smoothie Cake

- **For the Cake:**
    - 1 1/2 cups all-purpose flour
    - 1/2 cup sugar
    - 1/2 tsp baking powder
    - 1/2 tsp baking soda
    - 1/4 tsp salt
    - 1/2 cup mashed banana (about 1 large banana)
    - 1/2 cup fresh strawberries, chopped
    - 1/2 cup Greek yogurt
    - 1/4 cup milk
    - 1/4 cup vegetable oil
    - 1 large egg
    - 1 tsp vanilla extract
- **For the Frosting:**
    - 1/2 cup unsalted butter, softened
    - 1 cup powdered sugar
    - 2 tbsp milk
    - 1/4 cup strawberry puree

Instructions:

1. **Preheat Oven:** Preheat oven to 350°F (175°C). Grease and flour an 8-inch round cake pan.
2. **Prepare Batter:** In a bowl, whisk together flour, sugar, baking powder, baking soda, and salt. In another bowl, mix mashed banana, strawberries, yogurt, milk, oil, egg, and vanilla extract. Combine with dry ingredients and mix until smooth.
3. **Bake:** Pour batter into the prepared pan and bake for 25-30 minutes, or until a toothpick inserted into the center comes out clean. Cool completely.
4. **Prepare Frosting:** Beat butter until creamy. Gradually add powdered sugar, milk, and strawberry puree. Frost the cooled cake and serve.

www.ingramcontent.com/pod-product-compliance
Lightning Source LLC
LaVergne TN
LVHW081504060526
838201LV00056BA/2922